Carol Sissa

PROVERBS FROM THE NORTH

WORDS OF WISDOM
FROM THE VIKINGS

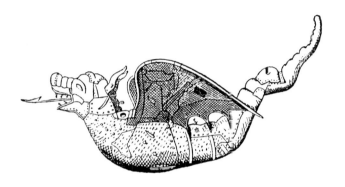

Translated from the Icelandic
by Joanne Asala

Illustrations from:
The Viking Age
by Paul B. Du Chaillu
Charles Scribner's Sons
1889

Penfield
Press

For my brother Ed, who has a Viking Spirit.

About the Editor
Joanne Asala is a writer and editor dedicated to the preservation of folklore and traditional customs. Of Finnish and Polish descent, she grew up in Bloomingdale, Illinois, and earned an English degree from the University of Iowa with an emphasis in Medieval literature. Her titles for Penfield Press include *Swedish Proverbs, Norwegian Proverbs, Czech Proverbs, Polish Proverbs, Trolls Remembering Norway,* and *Fairy Tales of the Slav Peasants and Herdsmen.* She is also the author of *Whistling Jigs to the Moon: Tales of Irish and Scottish Pipers* and *The Green Knight: A Tale of Ancient Britain.*

Acknowledgments
A special thank-you to Darrell Henning, Director, and Carol Hasvold, Librarian/Registrar, Vesterheim, The Norwegian-American Museum, Decorah, Iowa; and to Dr. Jon Wilcox, Dr. David Chamberlain and Dr. Valerie Lagorio, Professors of Medieval Literature, Dr. Harry Oster, Professor of Folklore, The University of Iowa.
Editorial Associates: John D. Zug, Dorothy Crum, Georgia Heald, Joan Liffring-Zug and Miriam Canter.
Graphic Design: Robyn Loughran.

Cover Illustration
Front: Odin and the wolf in a ritual dance. From a die from Torslunda, Sweden. Fifth Century. Back: warriors with boar-crested helmets. Torslunda, Sweden. Fifth Century.

Books by Mail
$10.95 each, postpaid to one address. Prices subject to change.
Words of Wisdom from the Vikings (this book)

Scandinavian Proverbs	Norwegian Proverbs
Swedish Proverbs	Danish Proverbs
Finnish Proverbs	Scottish Proverbs
Polish Proverbs	Czech Proverbs

For a complete catalog of titles please send $2.00 to:
Penfield Press
215 Brown Street
Iowa City, IA 52245

Illustration at top of page: Rectangular pendant of sheet gold with embossed human figure.

Table of Contents

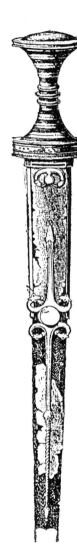

Iron Age sword with bronze handle. Found in a bog at Fremlöse, not far from the town of Odense, Denmark, with fragments of two other iron swords. The greater number of Viking Age swords were without silver inlay or any special treatment of the hilt. For the true warrior, the qualities of the blade were far more important.

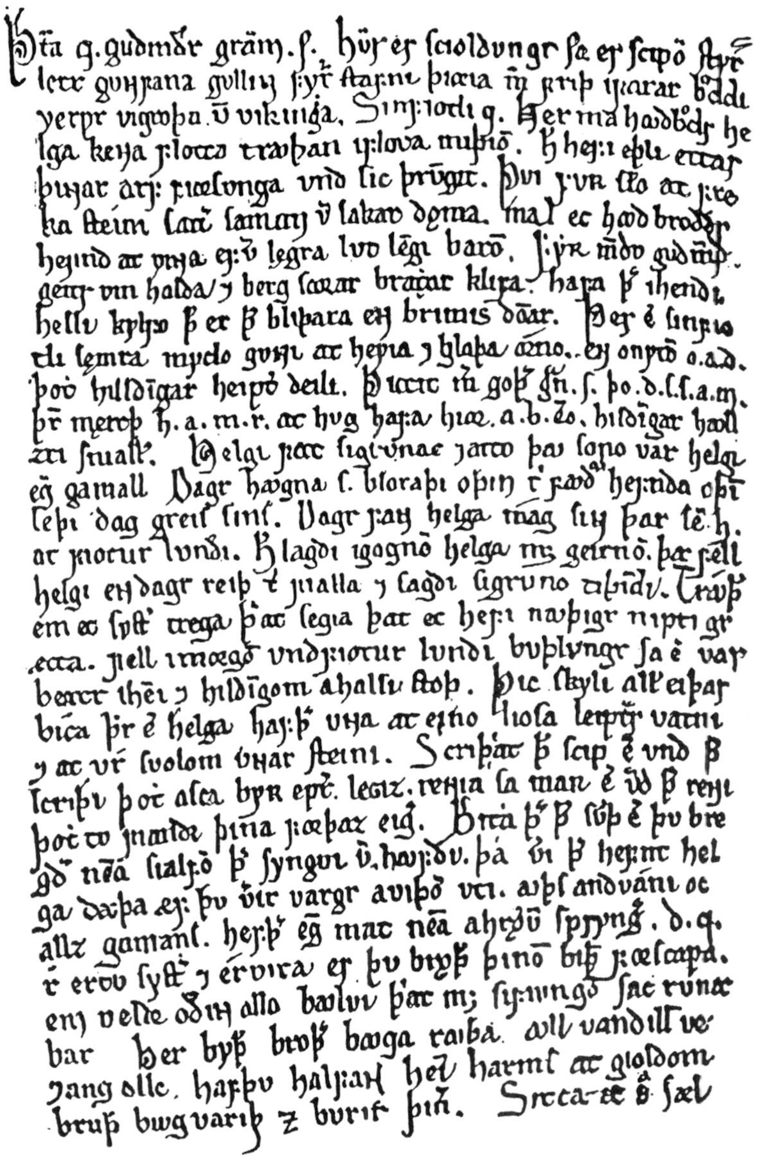

Complete page from *The Elder Edda*.

The Code of the Warrior

Silent and thoughtful should a warrior be,
and bold on the battlefield;
Cheerful and content should every man be,
until he meets his death.

This verse, and the others in the book, come from the
Hávámál, a compilation of Old Norse poems that offer the
reader a variety of practical advice, rules of conduct, and
words of wisdom. Said to be given by Odin, Father of the
Norse Gods, they represent a clear picture of the heroic
ethics, home life and warrior code of the Viking Period
(790AD–1070).

Vikings are typically thought of as savage, marauding
pirates who traveled the seas, terrorizing all those they
came in contact with. Yet the words of the *Hávámál* show
us a different side of the Vikings, a side that was con-
cerned with such issues as fairness, love and family.

In the early days of Viking expansion, the areas now
known as Sweden, Norway and Denmark had very fluid
frontiers. The people all spoke a similar language, Old
Norse, worshiped the same gods, and were primarily farm-
ers. Most of the countryside was a confusing patchwork of
petty states whose populations were made up of land-
holding aristocrats, slaves and freemen. Members of these
tribes eventually migrated to Iceland in 874, Greenland in
986, and Vinland the Good (North America) sometime
between 986 and 1011. They had base camps on nearly
every important waterway in western Europe, and large

Silver vase found in
Götland, Sweden.

settlements in England and Normandy. They sailed
through the Mediterranean, the Black Sea, the Baltic, and
the Atlantic, and perhaps considered their raiding as a
means of restocking their supplies and financing their next
expedition. The Vikings were definitely more than pirates.
They had a complex set of laws and a rich oral culture—a
culture and mythology lasting until around the year 1000,
when they adopted Christianity.

Although the words of the *Hávámál* are attributed to
Odin, there is no mention of life after death, of religious
belief, or of faith in the gods. The advice is very practical,
and applies to the everyday life of the "average Viking."
It seems there was more concern placed on winning honor
in this world than in achieving the afterlife, and a person's
most valuable possession was not his soul, but his good
name—the only thing that could outlive him.

Death was then the greatest evil, something to be avoid-
ed at all costs. The *Hávámál* gives all sorts of advice on
how to stay alive. In the end, however, death comes to all
men and women, and the one who faces death bravely is
the one who dies well.

Friendship is another important aspect of the *Hávámál*.
A man often placed his life in the hands of his comrades
and he needed to be certain of their loyalty. Therefore,
gold was not given to the son to inherit, but spent freely
on friends. The penalty for betrayal was death, and
vengeance was the noble course of action.

Ultimately, the *Hávámál* paints a picture of the ideal Viking: he must be open, friendly and generous; he must be wise—but not too wise—he must keep his wits about him and be ready for a fight; he must hold honor high and be loyal to friends and kin. In short, he must be the perfect hero.

So enjoy the thousand-year-old wisdom of the Vikings. Perhaps you will find these words speak to the Viking heart in each of us.

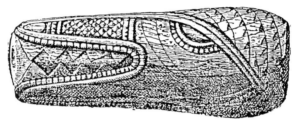

Crocodile's head carved in wood.

When is a Viking Not a Viking?

The name "Vikings" is a convenient term used when discussing the Scandinavian people of a certain era. These tribes did not think of themselves as "Vikings," nor were they called "Vikings" by their neighbors. To the Anglo-Saxons they were known as *Danes*, the Franks called them *Normanni* (Northmen), the Germans referred to them as *Ashmen*, the Irish as *Gaill* (Foreigners), the Spanish Arabs as *Majus* (Heathens), and the Slavs and Byzantine Greeks as *Rus*. The Scandinavians identified themselves as people of a certain region, for example, "Men of the Uplands." As national identities began to take shape, they saw themselves as "Northmen," later as Norwegians, Swedes and Danes. Each group went its own way, the Danes sailed the western seas, as did the Norwegians, while the Swedes went east. The word "Viking" is of obscure origin, and may have originally meant "Creek-Men."

A Note on the Hávámál

The *Hávámál* is part of a greater body of work known as
The Poetic Edda. Scholars do not agree on where the *Edda*
was written, or when. Some say that it was composed in
Iceland; others argue that it was written down in Britain or
Norway. These poems are most likely survivors of the oral
culture of the tenth century, but they were not written
down until the thirteenth century—and then by Christian
scribes who no longer entirely understood what they were
writing about. It was an Icelandic historian, Snorri
Sturluson (1179-1241) who first composed a book of
pre-Christian lore known as *The Prose Edda*. Other scribes,
who are anonymous, compiled fragments of ancient heroic
poetry, and today this collection is known as *The Elder* or
Poetic Edda. The oldest extant manuscript of this poetry is
the *Codex Regius*, now in Reykjavík, Iceland. It dates from
the late thirteenth century, but is believed to be a copy
from an original manuscript written sometime between
1210 and 1240.

Bracteate. Shows a figure of a man
and a two-horned animal. Now in
the Stockholm Museum, Sweden.

ENEMIES AND FOES

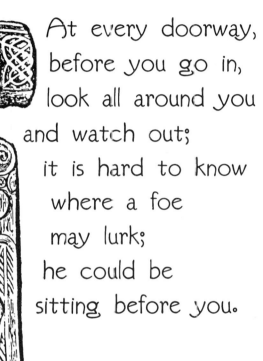

At every doorway,
before you go in,
look all around you
and watch out;
it is hard to know
where a foe
may lurk;
he could be
sitting before you.

Never tell a man
whom you don't trust
that you've fallen on
hard times.

If you think well of a
cruel man, you'll be
ill-rewarded.

When foes fight,
    courage is better
than the power
    of sword.

When evil befalls you,
    let it be known;
don't let your foe
    go free.

Damascened iron
sword of the later Iron
Age. Found in a bog
near Slagelse on
Sjælland, Denmark.

Griffin's head.
Ornament belonging
to helmet of bronze.

If you have
cause to
quarrel with
another,
be sure to fight in the
open; better to
challenge your foe now
than to have your home
set on fire.

A man may sit
at the feast in
friendly conversation
before he learns
he has dined
with foes.

HOSPITALITY

Hail to the host!
A guest is in the hall, where
shall the stranger sit down?
To make a new friend,
quickly give him
the bench
nearest the fire.

Chair carved with
fighting warriors.
The helmets on
their heads are
similar to those
found on the
Bayeux Tapestry.

Silver goblet, with repoussé work of silver plated with gold. The most common drink of the Viking Age was probably ale, although there are numerous references to mead. The Vikings also drank *beor*, a type of fruity wine.

The night
is friendly when
the food is plenty.

Scoff not
at the guest, nor
drive him to the door;
be kind to beggars!

A fire should be ready
for the frozen knees
of guests who come
to your hall.

It's good manners to
give your guest
conversation and
a chance to speak.

Food and dry
clothes are needed by
one who has traveled
over the mountain.

Listen carefully before
you judge a man
who comes to
your feast.

Don't ever mock
or laugh at a guest
or wayfarer.

Above: A ritual dance with two berserks
(warriors who changed into animals
before battle). Below: Sigurd about to
slay the dragon. Only fragments of cloth
from the Viking Age survive, and
reconstruction of Nordic costumes is
often based on artifacts such as these,
as well as picture stones and literary
descriptions.

TRAVEL AND ADVENTURE

Don't leave your
weapons behind
when you travel
in the open field,
for you never know
when on
the distant road
you may suddenly need
your spear.

Spears often had poetical names. Odin's spear was called *Gunguir*. Some other names were:

The Pole of Darrad (Odin)
The Sounding Fish of
   the Armor
The Snake of the Corpse
The Venom-Thong of
   the Fight
The Flying Dragon of
   the Wounds

The Thorn of
   the Wound
The Serpent of Blood
The Serpent of Battle
The Serpent of Wound
The Serpent of Shield
The Shooting Serpent
The Snake of the Attack

It takes sharp wits
to wander through
        the world.

If you travel over
mountain, gulf or fjord,
don't forget to
        put food in your pack.

Scene from the Bayeux Tapestry, embroidered in the 1070s to com-
memorate the defeat of the Anglo-Saxon king, Harold Godwinson, by
William the Conqueror at the Battle of Hastings in 1066.

Semi-spherical gold
ornamentation of
unknown use.

Wisdom is worth
more than gold
on an unknown path.

There is no gift
more valuable than fire,
no sight finer than
                    the sun.

A man must travel widely
before he has the
wisdom to see into
the heart of another.

If a man travels the road
with a head full of sense,
he can carry nothing
better.

Glass bead, mosaic bead, bead of gold and
silver, mosaic bead of red color.

Helmet of iron found in the decayed remains of a small ship buried in Ultuna Mound not far from Uppsala, Sweden. Helmets from the Viking Age were not horned, despite popular imagination.

Bracteate found in Trollhätten, Sweden.

Very frequently does the weather change in a week, and more in a month's time.

Don't trust
    the autumn night.

If you are wise,
you will not speak
with fools you meet
in your travels.

Winter's father
is called Cold Wind;
Summer's sire
        is Delight.

Bury the bodies
of the fallen
when you find them
in your travels,
whether they be
killed by disease or
drowned in the sea,
or slain on
the field of
battle.

Red quartz stone
with earlier runes
and warrior on
horseback. Height:
eight feet three inch-
es, but only six feet
are above ground.
Uppland, Sweden.

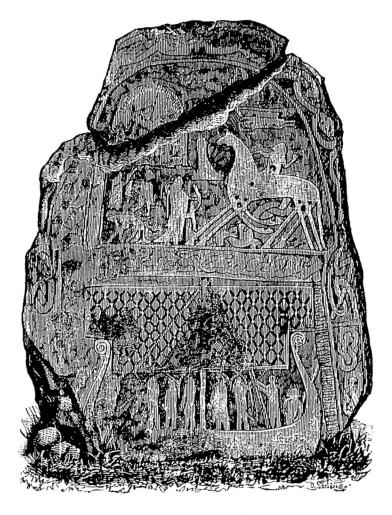

Picture stone from Tjängvide, Götland, Sweden.
The scene at the top shows the eight-footed
horse of Odin and the arrival of a dead hero in
Valhalla, the great hall of immortality in which
the souls of warriors slain heroically in battle
were received. Eighth or Ninth Century.

A Head Full of Wisdom

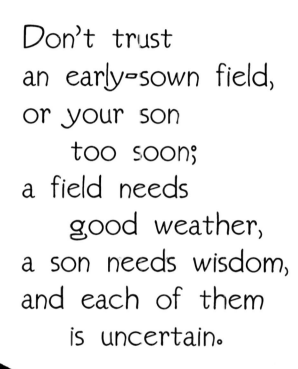

Don't trust
an early-sown field,
or your son
    too soon;
a field needs
    good weather,
a son needs wisdom,
and each of them
    is uncertain.

Various farm implements. Plow of oak wood found in Jutland, Denmark. Shears from Uppsala, Sweden. Sickles found in a grave mound along with burnt bones.

Stylized man's head on a piece of bronze covered with thin gold plate.

In the blink of an eye
the fool is discovered
when he sits
among the wise.

Trouble seldom comes
to the silent and wise.

A man will never find
a better friend than his
own common sense.

A fool needs but
a single drink
before the little wit
he has collapses.

This partially gilded silver cup comes from a large hoard deposited at the time of King Valdemar Atterdag's invasion of Götland, Sweden, in 1361. Eleventh Century.

Many seem clever
if they're asked
no questions.

When a foolish man
sits among others,
he'd best keep silent;
no one will know
that he knows nothing,
unless he talks too much.

Fibula of bronze.
On its pin was a
piece of linen. Found
with mosaic beads in
a stone coffin.

Moderately wise
should every man be,
don't seek to know
        too much;
for the heart of a man
        is seldom happy
if he is truly wise.

Mosaic beads.

25

On The Field of Battle

The foolish man
thinks he will live
      forever
if he shuns
the battlefield;
but old age
shows him no mercy,
though spears
      spare his life.

Various spear heads from sites
in Norway.

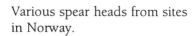

Bronze mounting, plated with gold-silver, and belonging to ring armor.

Don't look around you
in the midst of battle,
many is the man
gone mad with fear, and
an evil spell
may strike you.

Violence and words of hate
aren't soon forgotten,
nor is sorrow
quickly healed.

Ring mail from a
suit of armor.

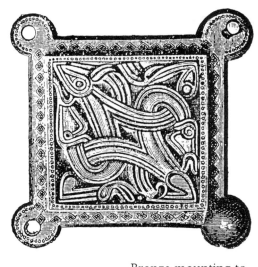

Bronze mounting to
a belt. Found when
plowing.
Götland, Sweden.

A warrior
needs wisdom
and strength
of arms if he wishes
to surpass his peers.

Do not trust
the word of a warrior
   if his brother is your enemy,
or if you've killed
            his father.

MEN AND WOMEN

I realized as I lay
    among the rushes,
waiting for the girl I loved,
that although she meant
    everything to me,
she was no more mine
for that.

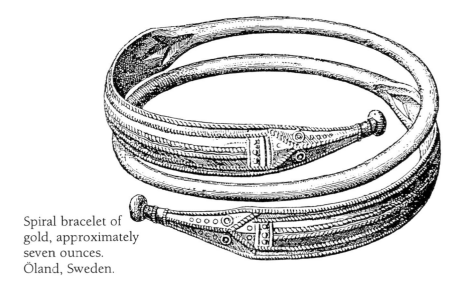

Spiral bracelet of
gold, approximately
seven ounces.
Öland, Sweden.

Do not let a pretty
face and the gleam of
finery keep you from a
good night's sleep.

Sport with a maiden
in the dark;
the day has many eyes.

For a wise man there is no
worse sickness than having
nothing to love.

To win a
maiden's love,
speak soft,
pleasing words,
offer wealth
and presents.

Pins found in a
cairn. Hemse,
Götland, Sweden.

So you will find the love
of a fickle-willed woman:
     like an unshod horse
     traveling over ice,
     a restless two-year-old
     not yet trained,
     or sailing without
     a rudder in a strong sea,
     or a lame man hunting
     reindeer on slippery rocks.

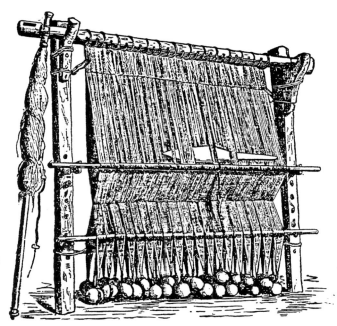

Ancient loom
from the Fäeroes
in the Bergen
Museum,
Norway.

He wins whose wooing is best.

Let no man ever
    ridicule another,
laughing at his love.

Never seduce
another man's wife
or long to be her love.

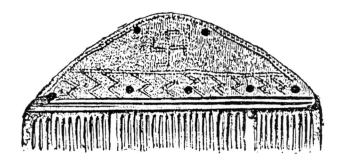

Descriptions of women and their finery abound in the Icelandic sagas. Above: Spiral gold ring alloyed with silver, showing the two sides. Below: Bone comb with *svastica*. The *svastica* has been a religious emblem of worldwide occurrence since at least 10,000 B.C. It was used as a magic sign in Europe up to the beginning of the Twentieth Century.

If you want to win
a maiden's love,
and keep her as
a friend,
make fair promises
and keep your pledge,
she'll love
what treasure
she gets.

Above:
Fibula of silver.
Below: Necklace
of gold, orna-
mented with
Roman and
Byzantine coins
of the Fifth Century.
Scania, Denmark. Now
in the Copenhagen
Museum, Denmark.

Viking Age jewelry.

Women always worry—
    this is not wisdom.

No one can speak
    with certainty
of what is possible
for people in love.

Don't tempt a maiden
or another's wife
with gifts
    or hints of pleasure.

A wicked woman
    often waits
      to blunt your wits
      and weapons.

MEAD

Mead isn't the blessing to men that many say it is; the more you drink the less you stay the master of your wits.

Silver cup from the Bavenhöi grave find.

From the Bayeux Tapestry, showing drinking horns and bowls similar to those found in Viking sites.

There is no greater
burden than a head
    that is heavy with ale.

It is the best of drinking,
if a man will soon come
to his senses again.

Ale and battle-words
are often a source
of sadness.

Don't argue with
drunken warriors;
    mead steals the
    minds of many.

Glass drinking horn, eight inches
in length. Diameter of mouth,
two and one half inches. Very
rare in the north. Bavenhöi grave
find.

CONDUCT IN THE HALL

To many halls
I came too early,
    to others much
    too late;
the ale was drunk
    or not yet brewed,
an unexpected guest
    finds no welcome.

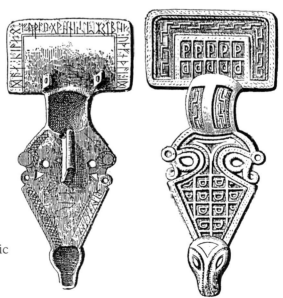

Fibula of silver,
partly gilt, with runic
letters. Burgundy,
France.

Don't cling to your ale,
but drink your measure;
speak to the point
or keep silent.

Carved doorway,
Sauland's Church,
Telemark, Norway.

Golden horn discovered in 1734. Originally it must have been over twenty inches long, and weighed more than eight pounds

No one will blame you
for being rude
if you go to bed early.

Unless he has
some sense,
a greedy man
will eat
until he's ill.

The herds know
when it's time to
give up their grazing
and go home.

Love turns to loathing
if you sit too long
by someone else's fire.

When the poor man is in
the rich man's hall,
he is wise to
        watch what he says;
boastful words are
not heard in the
hall of a selfish host.

No one can keep
anything concealed
once it is heard
        in the hall.

Nothing will ever
bring to an end
the strife of guests
        at meals.

Gold horn
discovered in
1639, with thirteen
broad rings round
it. Length, two feet
nine inches; weight,
over seven pounds.

40

Don't be
hungry when
you ride to
    the council,
be clean though
your clothes be poor,
do not be ashamed
by shoes and breeches,
nor by your horse,
though he be
    no champion.

FRIENDSHIP

Crooked and far
is the path to a foe,
though his house lies
next to yours;
but it's no great
distance to
a friend, though
it's many miles
to his door.

Hiberno-Saxon mount
with Viking Age swords,
found in a grave at
Myklebostad, Norway.

I've never met a
man so generous of his
wealth that he would not
accept a gift.

Give gifts to your friends,
they are
   as happy as you
to wear new weapons
   and clothes.

A man should be
a friend to his friend,
   giving gift for gift;
laughter should be returned
   for laughter, lying for lies.

Above: Box with top open in which
there was a scale, ten beads, and
two ornaments of silver. Petes,
Götland, Sweden.

A man should keep
faith with his friends,
and to the
        friends of friends,
but no man should
extend a hand
        in friendship
to the friend of a foe.

The exchange of gifts
makes friendship last
if they are given
with good will.

The foolish man thinks
everyone his friend
        who smiles
        when he does;
but he learns the truth
when he comes to the
council and few speak
in his favor.

Scabbard of bronze
and iron knife found
in a tumulus mound
along with a skele-
ton. Rikirde,
Götland, Sweden.

Rich did I feel
when a comrade I found,
   no man is happy alone.

With half a loaf
and a cup of ale,
I have found
many a friend.

The fir tree withers
on the bare hillside
without needles or bark;
it is like a man
whom no one loves—
no need for his life
to be long.

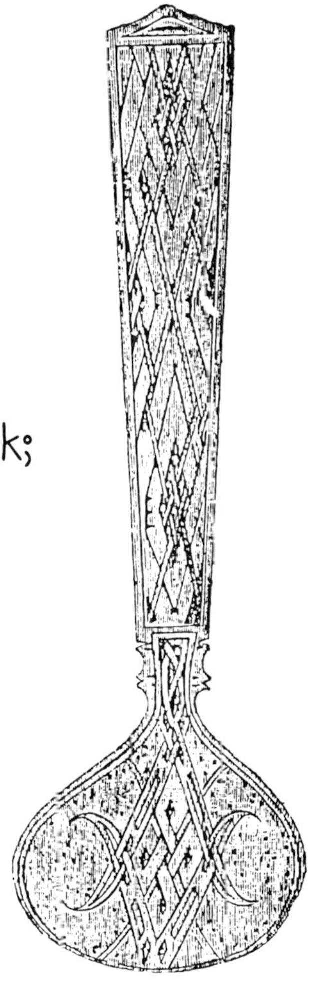

Spoon of Elkhorn
found in the black earth
in Björke, Sweden.

Wealth is as swift as
the blink of an eye,
wealth is the
falsest of friends.

Bronze buckle found
in a small cairn at
Hemse, Götland,
Sweden.

If you have a friend,
go see him often;
brushwood and grass will soon
grow tall on the road
which no one walks.

Sorrow eats the heart of one
who cannot reveal his
mind to another.

Gold fibula inlaid with colored
glass. Found in a copper box in the
ground, with necklaces, bracelets,
finger rings and over 4,000 coins of
German, English and Swedish mint.
Blekinge, Sweden.

46

A good man will help
you achieve favor
and fortune.

Anything is better than
a broken friendship.

A true friend
will speak words
you'd rather not hear.

Good men come to
grief when an evil man
wields his sword.

Various bracteates. From top to bottom: Warrior with
sword, fighting animals; bracteate with *svastica* and
dots on it, warrior's head with helmet over the face;
man's head with symbolic signs; man on horseback.

BE IT EVER SO HUMBLE

Even if it's a hut,
it's better to have
a house you can
    call your own;
with just a goat and
a straw-thatch roof,
you're better off
    than begging.

Even if it's a hut,
it's better to have
a house you can
    call your own;
a man's spirit breaks if
he's forced to beg
    for his daily bread.

Top: Key with chain, Hemse,
Götland, Sweden.
Bottom: Key of bronze, Norway.

EARLY TO BED & EARLY TO RISE

Get up early if you have
few workers and attend
to the chore yourself.
Much remains undone while
      you lie in bed;
work is half one's wealth.

Get up early if you
seek another man's
life or property.

A sleeping wolf
will rarely make a kill,
nor an idle warrior
win fame.

Brooch of silver and
cloisonné enamel.
Seventh Century.

A MAN'S REPUTATION

Cattle die, kinsmen die,
one day you too will die;
but a noble name
will never perish
when a man earns
praise and fame.

Harald Bluetooth's rune stone at Jelling, Denmark, c.965. It was erected when Christianity was introduced to Denmark. An inscription reads, "King Harald had these memorials made to Gorm his father and to Thyre his mother. That Harald who won for himself all Denmark and Norway and made the Danes Christian."

Happy is the man who
has earned for himself
    wisdom and
    words of praise.

Men generous and noble
    live the best lives;
seldom do they feel
                sorrow.

A man will get his just
    reward for the words
he speaks to others.

Drum-shaped brooch of bronze
with gildings of silver and gold.
From Mårtens, Götland,
Sweden. Eleventh Century.

Better to have a son,
though he be born
when you're buried;
the only memorial stones
are those placed by kin.

It is hard to know
    what may be hidden
    in another man's heart.

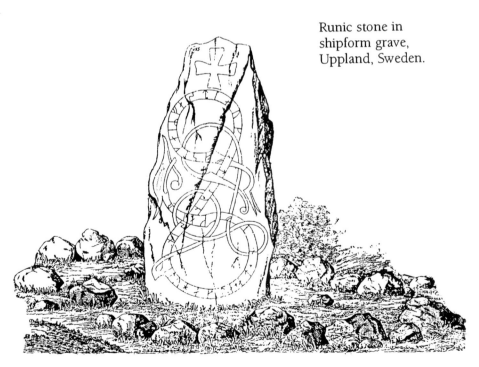

Runic stone in
shipform grave,
Uppland, Sweden.

One man is wealthy
and another poor;
blame not a man
for that.

Only you can know
what dwells
near your heart;
a man alone knows
his mind.

No man is so good
that he is without fault,
nor so bad that he is
good for nothing.

It is better to try than
be called a coward,
if you want
to do the deed.

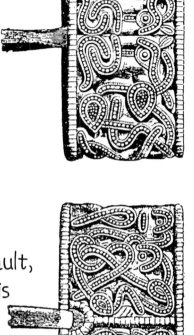

Ornaments for the
mouthpiece of a
scabbard as seen
from both sides. The
two sides are never
the same.

Don't give your kin
reason to reproach you;
don't be too eager
to seek revenge
though the dead
deserve it.

If a bridle
    is not found,
a babbling tongue
    will do you
        damage.

Top: Bronze mount
from the decorated
end of a harness
bow. Mid Sixth-
Century, Denmark.
Bottom: Spur and
parts of a harness.

Evil counsel has
often come from
a jealous man's heart.

Never swear an oath
you cannot keep—
bitter is the payment
for broken promises.

When accusations are
brought against you,
do not keep silent,
otherwise men will say
you're a coward,
or worse,
        believe the lie.
Later, cut off the liar's
life with your sword.
Deceit deserves
        such justice!

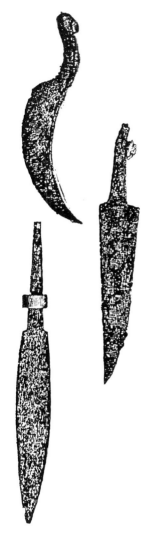

Curved iron knife,
found with the
remains of a large
urn containing burnt
bones. Iron knives
found in a cinerary
urn containing burnt
bones, two pairs of
shears, and a broken
awl.

It's better to be blind
than buried,
   dead men do no deeds.

Do not flee,
though death is certain,
unless you wish to be
   called a coward.

One of two wagons found in the Deiberg Bog,
Ringkjobing, West Jutland, Denmark.
Ornamented all over with bronze. Each side
has representations of two human heads with
heavy mustaches, triskele and other mystic
signs. Length of sides, five foot, four inches;
diameter of wheels, three feet.

SAGE ADVICE

A creaking bow, a burning flame,
a yawning wolf, a croaking crow,
a grunting boar, a rootless tree,
a waxing wave, a bubbling kettle,
a flying arrow, a falling tide,
newly formed ice, a coiled snake,
the pillow-talk of a bride
     or a broken sword,
a bear at play or a king's son,
a sick calf, a stubborn slave,
a flattering witch, a newly felled foe,
your brother's killer,
     even if met on the free road,
a half-burned house
or a horse full swift,
a man has
too much faith
     to trust in these.

Bronze kettle, Norway. Found under a
slab in the border around a mound. It
contained burnt bones, among which was
a gold bracelet and other objects.

57

Bracteates forming part of a necklace, found at Faxö, Sjælland, Denmark.

A man should spend
his hard-earned money
on whatever
his own needs are.

The men who live
the fairest lives
    know just a
    few things well.

No man ought to know
his fate beforehand,
then his mind is free
from care.

A wise man learns from
the counsel of others;
a fool prefers his own.

Tell one your thoughts,
but don't tell two;
        all know what is
        known to three.

A man must be
watchful, and wary as well,
and fearful of trusting
a stranger.

Top: Ring with charms
representing a sword, a
spearhead, and some
Arabic coins. Öland,
Sweden.
Right: Box of bronze
found in a mound.
Sjælland, Denmark.

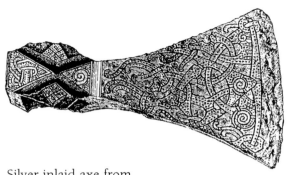

Silver inlaid axe from Mammen, Jutland, Denmark, late Tenth Century. From a richly furnished man's grave. In the Viking Age, silver-inlaid axes were status symbols for the most prominent men. This man no doubt belonged to the court of Harald Bluetooth.

Praise the day at sunset,
a woman on her pyre,
a sword tried
          and tested,
a maiden married,
ice when it is crossed,
ale when it is drunk.

Trees should be cut
when the wind blows;
in fair weather
sail on the sea.

Seek swiftness from a ship,
protection from a shield,
cuts from a sword,
     kisses from a maiden.

60

Buy a steed that is lean
and a sword that is
blood-stained.

Don't wear shoes,
or use carved spears,
unless you've made
        them yourself;
an ill-fitting shoe
or a crooked shaft
leads to evil luck.

Don't take joy in
wicked deeds;
    be happy when
    you do good.

Various tools from
the Viking Age:
tongs, pincer,
hammerhead.

Be careful with ale,
and another man's wife,
and don't let thieves
play you tricks.

Better no prayers
than too great
              an offering;
better no sacrifice
than one too large.

Gold ornament of a
sword belt.

Beware of the wolf
in your young son,
    gladly he takes
          your gold.

Do not commit evil
acts; keep away
from what is false.

Resources and Recommended Reading

Beckett, Samuel. *The Fjords and Folk of Norway*.
Methuen & Company. London, 1915.

Bellows, Henry. *The Poetic Edda*. American
Scandinavian Foundation. New York, 1923.

Boer, R.C., editor. *The Edda*. Haarlem, 1922.

Cohat, Yves. *The Vikings, Lords of the Sea*.
Abrams, Incorporated. New York, 1992.

D'Aulaires, Ingri & Edgar. *Norse Gods and Giants*.
Doubleday. New York, 1967.

Evans, Cheryl & Millard, Ann. *Norse Myths and Legends*.
Usborne Publishers. London, 1986.

Foote, P.G. *The Viking Achievement*. Praeger Publishers.
New York, 1970.

Hollander, Lee M. *The Poetic Edda*. University of Texas Press.
Austin, 1928.

Möbius, Theodor. *Edda Sæmunder*. Leipzig 1860.

Munch, Peter Andreas. *Den Ældre Edda*. Christiania, 1847.

Neckel, Gustav, editor. *The Song of the Codex Regius*.
Heidelberg, 1927.

Oxenstierns, Eric. *The World of the Norsemen*. World Publishing.
Cleveland, 1967.

Philpotts, Bertha. *The Elder Edda*. Cambridge University Press.
Cambridge, 1920.

Sijmons, B. *Die Lieder der Edda*. Halle, 1888.

Simpson, Jacqueline. *Everyday Life in the Viking Age*.
G.P. Putnam and Sons. New York, 1967.

Terry, Patricia. *Poems of the Vikings*. Macmillan. New York, 1986.

Young, Jean, translator. *The Prose Edda*. Berkeley, 1966.

Zöega, Geir. *A Concise Dictionary of Old Icelandic*.
Oxford University Press. Oxford, 1961.

Viking ship used for burial.
Gokstad, Norway.